I have always felt most beautiful · There is no greater feeling of security than the knowledge that I am passionately loved by my Father, God. Out of that knowledge springs a radiance no amount of lipstick can conjure. Deborah's "Moments of Meditation" point so clearly to Him, the true Source of all beauty and radiance.

Dana Embree
Pastor's wife, Crossroads Church, mother

How we look, think, speak, and act models the very essence of who we are, what we believe, and what our life purpose is. Deborah models grace while acknowledging a person's presence and unvoiced questions: Do you see me? Do you hear me? Do you care about what I think and feel? She takes time to listen to God, and her beautifully written, God-inspired book lays out a step-by-step process to hear His voice.

Frankie Walters
President, Frankie Walters Personal and Professional Development,
wife, mother, grandmother

Deborah reminds us that God has designed our lives and that He has a plan for our lives, no matter how old we are. As we age, the media leads us to believe we are no longer beautiful. The beauty industry tries to sell us products to maintain or regain our beauty. Our lives are gifts from God. His love helps to make us beautiful from the inside out. The lines on our faces are gentle reminders of the wonderful lives He has given us. Physical beauty may fade, but kindness and love are beautiful forever.

Sandi Galloway
Director, Southwest Sales Development, widow

Have you ever met a woman and you weren't sure why you were captivated by her presence? You just found yourself drawn in, like a moth to the light. Maybe she, like Esther, has prepared and made herself beautiful for the King's entrance. If we take time for our body, soul, and spirit to be whole, we will find true beauty and will be highly favored by our King. Mrs. King says that real beauty creates mystery and leaves something to be uncovered, and this is so true. It is more than lipstick! It is Him, King Jesus!

Jan Mayfield
Wife, mother, grandmother

Hopelessness, defeat, fear, and despair wrapped their tentacles around me, almost leaving me breathless. I was eight years old and failed the third grade. As a result, I believed I was dumb and stupid. I allowed thoughts of "dumb and stupid" to define my life, and I believed I would be that way forever.

Years later, in my early thirties, during a time of Bible study and prayer, I sensed the Holy Spirit breathing His life and truth into my heart. As I read the book of Genesis, I realized I was made in God's image.

That God-breathed truth set me free! I sensed the Holy Spirit hovering around me, holding me close, saying, "There are no failures in My kingdom; there are only experiences."

I wish I'd had the wisdom in Deborah's book all those years ago. It might have saved me from an emotional train-wreck.

Gail Patterson
Marriage Challenge Ministry, wife, mother, grandmother

These wise words, which Deborah has so beautifully written, show us that Jesus alone gives us lasting value and purpose in every season of life, especially during transitional or unclear times. Like Esther, we, too, can use the in-between time to prepare for what's ahead by recalibrating our thoughts to His. His truth takes the hurried, anxious, scrambling thoughts and replaces them with security.

Donna Sandberg
Pastor, City Church, wife, mother

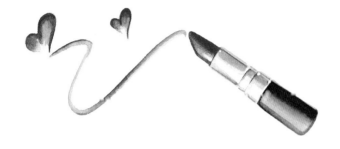

More Than Lipstick
You Are a Designer Original

Embrace your beautiful design

Debora

DEBORAH KING

ISBN: 978-1505949636

Library of Congress Control Number: 2013955716

Illustrations: Raphaela Anna Wilson
Cover Design: Anneli Anderson, www.designanneli.com
Interior Design: Raphaela Anna Wilson, boundless-creative.com
First Printing, Interior Design: Inside-Out Design & Typesetting, Hurst, TX

Printed in the United States of America
13 14 15 16 17 18 MG 6 5 4 3 2

Dedication

$\mathcal{M}$y life is a reflection of all I have learned from the many amazing women who have crossed my path—women who have modeled kindness, sacrificial love, wisdom, and unending patience. While the list alone could fill this book, one woman silently modeled the beauty, grace, and love of God to me at a pivotal time in my life: Shirley DeVore. Shirley, thank you for instilling in me what really matters in life. Your kitchen was the classroom. Your actions were the lessons. Your heart molded mine, as it has so many others.

"Being female is a matter of birth;

being a woman is a matter of age;

but being a lady is a matter of choice."

DEBORAH KING

Contents

Contents

Special Thanks

*Y*ou would not be holding this book without the help of so many beautiful women who grace my life with their wisdom and friendship. Terry Schurman, Lori DeVore, Jan Mayfield, Sara McPeek, Susan Parks, Dana Embree, Linda Savage, Monica Brandner, Donna Sandberg, Frankie Walters, Carrie Abbott, Gail Patterson, Tia Warren, Nancy Smith, Sandi Galloway, Keitha Story-Stephenson, Bethany Siggins, Debbie Willis, and Catherine Bell, thank you for your endless encouragement.

Raphaela Anna Wilson, words cannot express my gratitude for all you do for me. I am humbled by the images you have created for this book. Thank you for sharing your artistic gift with us all.

Introduction

*H*ave you ever noticed how a little girl exudes joy and confidence as she shamelessly dances and poses for anyone with a camera? She freely celebrates her beauty.

Sadly, the truth about her beautiful design is often marred at a very young age by lies that she is not good enough, she is not smart enough, she is not pretty enough; and slowly, her confidence diminishes, her innocence is tarnished, and she begins to hide.

God placed within us the desire for beauty! Everywhere we look we see His beautiful design. From the richness of a magnificent sunrise or sunset, to the stars in the night sky, the earth is filled with His beauty. He made the butterflies, the snowflakes, and the fall leaves; each individually unique and perfectly exquisite. No detail was too small, insignificant or overlooked in God's design.

As God so lovingly created our surroundings, He has also created you and me; each of us unique and exquisite in His eyes. Our Father God sees the beauty in us, but it is often difficult for us to see that same beauty within ourselves. Just as the young girl grows to lose confidence in her God-given beauty, many women lose the joy of feeling beautiful.

Introduction

I believe every woman longs to see beauty, not only in her daily surroundings, but in the reflection she sees in her mirror each morning. What makes a woman feel beautiful? Is it the perfect cosmetic or beauty product, the ideal outfit, secrets to a great personality, or an ivy-league education? Are these the things that make a woman feel beautiful and provide her with a sense of purpose? Rediscovering my own beautiful design has not come easily or quickly; in fact, it has been a life-long process.

In these pages, I will share with you some of the insights I have learned as I have embraced God's truth about my design. Through His Word and time spent in prayer, He has restored to me His truth of who I am and who I was created to be.

This is not another to-do list to add to your busy schedule; rather, it is an invitation to celebrate your beautiful design. This book is written in short sections to allow you to capture those few moments in your day while you sip your favorite beverage, wait for an appointment, your child takes a nap, or you have dinner simmering, to allow God to dress you in the truth of who He has created you to be: His beautiful daughter. At the end of each section, I have provided questions for you to consider, as well as scriptural references from the Bible for further reading. You may wish to answer the questions and write your study notes in my *More Than Lipstick Journal.*

Join me now as we discover together that real beauty is more than lipstick.

Deborah King

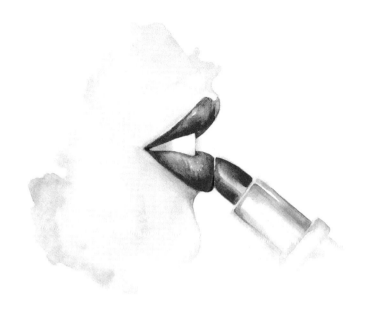

More Than Lipstick

The most versatile lipstick you can own is a shade
that's just a bit brighter than your natural lip color.
BOBBI BROWN

$\mathcal{R}$ed, peach, plum, pink, coral, fuchsia, mocha—women are absolutely in love with lipstick. So much so, they spend millions of dollars every year on it. Add in the enormous quantity of lip gloss and lip balm purchased each year, and there is no denying women are passionate about enhancing their lips.

This is not a new obsession. For centuries women have found

ways to beautify their lips. Lipstick has been used to indicate social and economic status, purity (or the lack thereof), strength, and beauty. While the meaning of wearing lipstick has changed over time, its use has endured.

During times when lipstick was reserved for those who lived unsavory lifestyles, more respectable women discovered other ways to enhance their lips, such as kissing rosy crepe paper, biting their lips, and even creating underground rouge societies.

What is the fascination with lipstick? Simply put, women like how a simple tube of lipstick can make them look and feel fabulous.

Throughout time, women have searched for ways to enhance their appearance and to feel beautiful, but true beauty is far more than applied lipstick. True beauty reaches into the depths of who you have been created to be. It encompasses so much more than the results of the newest miracle-working facial cream or a popular hair treatment. His beauty can be seen in the reflection you view in your mirror each morning as you truly embrace every aspect of who you are.

God, in His infinite wisdom, gave you the desire to see and appreciate beauty. He wants you to know and believe in the beauty He designed when He made you. You are a uniquely crafted, intricately detailed creation of Almighty God, and He wants you to know that He never makes mistakes.

More Than Lipstick

Moments of Meditation

What is your favorite beauty product? Why?

How do you define true beauty?

What makes you feel beautiful?

Good Morning, Beautiful

Live each day in a manner that encourages
others to do better and be better.

DEBORAH KING

I love mornings! It has always been a mystery to me why someone would want to exchange a little more time to sleep for the opportunity to see a new day spring to life. But then, I am a morning person.

I am one of those women who enjoys getting dressed for the day. While some of my friends have mastered the ten-minute face and can be out the door in minutes, I enjoy a more leisurely process. In fact, I love the time in the morning when I apply my makeup, style my hair, and select the clothes and accessories I will wear.

It is during this time I fix my heart on God and still my mind to hear Him speak to me. Some days He gives me direction. On other days, we simply sit together and *be*.

Among all the things God and I share, the consistent morning message I hear Him whisper to my heart is, *You were born for a time such as this. Before the foundation of the world, I made you, and I made you with a plan and purpose. I designed every aspect of who you are—the way you look, the things you love, where you live, and even the people I have placed in your life. Every detail is part of My design.* I cannot think of a more beautiful message, and it is one I need to hear every day.

Each morning, as I prepare for my day, I have a fresh opportunity to celebrate who He is and who He has created me to be. As true as this message is for me, the same is true for you. Every aspect of your life, the way you look, the things you love, where you live, and even your relationships, are all part of His design for you. I believe God has a morning message for you, and as you allow yourself time to listen, you will be filled with His peace and direction for your day.

Moments of Meditation

What time of day do you enjoy?

Describe your morning routine.

How does your morning routine set the tone for the rest of the day?

Preparation

Spectacular achievement is always
preceded by unspectacular preparation.
ROBERT H. SCHULLER

Preparation takes time. Esther, a Jewish orphan, who was brought up by her uncle Mordecai, understood the value and importance of preparation.

The Bible tells the story of King Xerxes, who banished Queen Vashti from his presence when she refused to display her beauty to all of his guests. During his search for a new queen, all the beautiful young ladies were forcefully taken from their homes and brought to the palace to prepare for the royal pageant.[1]

Unlike those in today's culture of expecting instant success, Esther patiently and faithfully prepared for an entire year for the time she would stand before the king. During that time, she learned the royal secrets of beauty and behavior.

Can you imagine a year of non-stop beauty treatments at the Ritz-Carlton or learning the qualities of royalty at Final Touch Finishing School? A year of daily facial, body and hair treatments? Learning how to walk, dress, speak, and master the protocol of the palace? Sounds like fun at first, but like anything else, it would eventually become work!

I can only imagine how lonely Esther felt during that year of preparation. She may have doubted herself and probably felt very afraid. All the dreams she held as a child evaporated the day she was taken from her family and friends. Faced with an uncertain future, she had to draw upon all she had been taught.

Esther had to do what was right, even when it was not easy. She knew if she did not prepare, she would not be ready when her moment came to stand before the king.

Rather than feeling entitled to the next promotion, the weight loss you desire, or the financial increase you dream of, what steps can you take now to ensure your success? Preparation is a life-long experience which involves formal education, learning from experts in their field, gaining advice from trusted mentors and personal study. As you take the daily steps to prepare yourself, God's favor will be at work on your behalf.

Moments of Meditation

Have you ever taken a class to learn etiquette or how to dress? If so, what did you learn? How did it change your social experience?

If not, how did you learn the appearance and social skills you know?

Have you experienced a time of preparation? What were you preparing for? What were the steps you took to prepare?

Study and Prepare

I will study and get ready,
and perhaps my chance will come.
ABRAHAM LINCOLN

Two principles I try to live by are to *study* and to *prepare*, and when I am ready, my time will come. These practices benefit my life in two very important ways.

First, when I feel anxious that nothing seems to be progressing in a particular area of my life, I remind myself to use that time to study and prepare. Rather than fretting, I focus on learning the skills I will need in the future.

Next, when faced with an opportunity I don't feel I am ready for, I remind myself—and God—that I have studied and prepared. I can have confidence and trust that His timing is perfect and He will provide.

Too often, rather than use our time wisely, we wrap ourselves in our comfort zone and live our lives on auto-pilot. Have you ever driven home and wondered how you got there? Auto-pilot causes you to travel the same route each day, you eat the same foods, go to the same places, do the same things and connect with the same people day after day. That sense of sameness causes you to live life without experiencing it, and keeps you overlooking opportunities to better yourself.

I love the example God has given us through the life of Esther. Although it seemed nothing was happening, Esther was not passively waiting for the day she would go before the King. She was busy preparing for whatever God had preordained. Due to her diligence and preparation, God was able to use Esther to save her whole nation.

Are you simply waiting for God to do something in your life? Or are you preparing yourself, so when He brings an opportunity to you, you will be ready?

More Than Lipstick

Moments of Meditation

How do you handle new opportunities you may not feel ready to face?

What are you doing today to prepare for your future?

My Moment

Every action should move you to a higher purpose.
DEBORAH KING

*W*hen I was seventeen years old, I was encouraged to compete in the local Miss America pageant. Without any training or preparation to be a pageant contestant, I agreed to enter the competition.

To my delight and surprise, I won first runner-up. While some may see that as second place, it was a win to me because, as the first runner-up, I went on to participate in the Seafair festivities in Seattle, Washington where I grew up.

Every summer since the 1950's, Seattle, has showcased its beauty and diversity with community festivals, parades, marine events, pageants, pirate appearances, air shows, and boat races. Miss Seafair is selected from the local pageant contestants for her friendliness, poise, speaking ability, and wholesomeness. She, King Neptune, and the Royal Court make their grand debut as the stars of the Torchlight Parade.

As a little girl, I had watched the regal waves of the Seafair royalty as they rode down the streets of Seattle during the evening Torchlight Parade. I secretly practiced my wave and dreamed of such a night. Now it would become my reality.

On the night of the Seafair Ball, as one of the local royalty, I walked into the banquet room dressed in my gown, sash, and crown, with my handsome escort at my side. The room was magnificent! The beautifully set tables danced with candlelight. I had never seen such an opulent setting.

In that moment, I was frozen with fear. I knew I was expected to know what to do, but had no idea where to begin. I was not raised in a family or an environment that taught me how to navigate the basic skills needed to lend confidence to this amazing opportunity. As a modeling school drop-out, I had developed only a limited amount of visual poise and image training. Sadly, I don't recall anything else about that night. I did, however, determine that I would learn the skills I needed so I would never again be intimidated by a knife, a fork, and a glass.

As the month of Seafair festivities came to a close, I sensed God giving birth to something far greater—His design for my life. He was gently leading me, preparing me, and directing me into the path He had created for me. Those skills I so desired to cultivate would become my life's greatest passion.

The skills you desire may not have been part of your early education, but they are something you can acquire. How can you nurture the talents God has placed within you? This is an important part of your preparation and crucial for future growth. Every time you use your talents, you are able to polish your current skills, identify skills you need to acquire and demonstrate your faithfulness.

More Than Lipstick

Moments of Meditation

What gifts and talents do others see in you?

What gifts do you see in yourself?

What are your areas of interest or passion?

Are you using your gifts? Where and how? If you are not, what is holding you back?

Social Skills

Modest dress, behavior, and speech never leave regret.
DEBORAH KING

*A*dvancing your education and developing the necessary skills to be excellent at your trade is an essential part of your preparation. While developing your technical expertise is important, developing strong social skills is also essential. Too often social skills are over-looked. Many assume these skills should just come naturally, like breathing. Others think they are simply niceties.

Social skills include the ABCs: appearance, behavior, and communication. They require training and focused attention, such as the skills required to read, play the piano, or be a great athlete. No one is born knowing how to dress and groom appropriately; meet and greet others with ease; carry on polite conversation; navigate through a multi-course meal; move with poise, grace, and confidence; or entertain with style.

These skills must be learned, and the person with the strongest social skills will garner favor and opportunities which surpass those given to the person with strong technical, but poor social skills.

Many people are *diamonds in the rough*. They have an unpolished exterior which appears rough and not worthy of notice, but underneath is the most beautiful gem. As a diamond needs to be cut, shaped and polished in the hands of an expert, so do we. Can you think of areas in your life which need to be shaped and polished?

If you feel you are lacking in some area, most often, you simply have not been properly trained in the skills needed for you to truly shine. With a little effort and some expert knowledge, you can learn the skills needed to stand out. Not only will you find you are no longer being overlooked, but you will walk into every situation with confidence and ease.

More Than Lipstick

Moments of Meditation

What academic or technical training have you acquired?

What social skills training have you acquired?

In what areas might you need to pursue some training? How would you go about getting that training?

What doors might open for you if you were to pursue that training?

Appearance

It is a powerful and memorable experience to be
in the presence of a true lady or gentleman.
DEBORAH KING

Your appearance is like an instant messaging system. In the blink of
an eye, people may determine many things about who you are, what
you believe, and how you live. In that brief moment, people decide if
you are the type of person they would like to get to know better.

It seems that image is an area in which women tend to lean
toward one of two ditches. In one ditch, vanity rules and individual

worth is based on one's appearance. In the other ditch, image doesn't matter at all. The only thing that matters is the condition of the heart.

Neither ditch is desirable. The goal is to walk consistently down the middle of the road, where you seek to embrace God's perspective about your image. You are created in His image, and His beautiful design includes your body, soul, and spirit.

In order to embrace your image, you need to know who you are. A good understanding of *your* style, *your* body type, and *your* coloring is invaluable. When you meet a new person, what will your appearance tell them about who *you* are? When you dress in agreement with your authentic self, others will have a clear insight into who you are.

While this is not a comprehensive study on this subject, here is a quick overview regarding Style Types, Body Types and Color.

STYLE TYPES:

Most of us fall into one of four basic categories. This is not to say you are only one of the four, but most of us have a tendency to lean more heavily towards one than the others.

- *Classic or Preppy:* Tailored, timeless accessories, polished, conservative make-up and hair.
- *Romantic or Feminine:* Flowing fabrics, ruffles and bows, delicate accessories, soft dewy make-up and longer hair.

- *Natural or Athletic:* Comfortable, natural fabrics, minimal accessories, natural looking make-up and carefree hair.
- *Dramatic or Artistic:* High fashion, unique combinations, bold accessories, exaggerated make-up and cutting-edge hair.

It is important to know which style best suits your personality and keep what is currently popular to a minimum when making major purchases.

BODY TYPES:

If you are like most women, there will always be something about your body that you don't love. The truth is this: although no one has a perfect body, we can cherish and care for the body God has given us.

I like to use the following four body types when helping women dress to their best advantage:

- X - Fuller top and bottom, with a narrow waist.
- H - Bust, hips and waist evenly proportioned.
- V - Fuller shoulders and bust, with narrow hips.
- A - Narrow shoulders and bust, with wider hips.

God created us to appreciate balance in all things. The most important tip I can give you is this: Never repeat a line you do not want to emphasize. (Example: If you have wider hips, never put a large, wide belt around that area of your body.)

When you understand which of the listed body types is closest to your shape, you can dress in a way that creates an illusion of balance. Your confidence will increase as you learn to dress and love the body you have.

Color:

The colors you choose to wear will play a large part in the image you create because our eyes see color first. When you select colors that are in harmony with your skin, hair and eyes, you will be the focus and appear more attractive. The wrong colors will cause you to look drab and even, at times, sickly.

I would like to share a few thoughts to consider when choosing the correct colors to enhance your natural beauty. First, it is important to note that there are three palates to look at when identifying your personal coloring:

- Warm: this color palate consists of yellow based colors.
- Cool: this color palate consists of blue based colors.
- Neutral: this color palate is not strongly warm or cool.

Next, you will sparkle when you can match your eye color (or the flecks of color in your eye) with the clothing closest to your face. And lastly, consider the level of contrast between your hair, skin and eyes. Light skin and dark hair have high contrast which enables you to wear clothing that duplicates that contrast, like black and white.

More Than Lipstick

When you prepare for your day, consider where you will be going, who you will be meeting, and what your goals are for that day. Then select the clothing which will best communicate your message. Your appearance is your best calling card. You can open doors or miss important opportunities just by how you look.

Take time over your daily grooming, making sure your skin, hair, and nails are well tended. Keep your clothing clean, well pressed and neat looking. Nothing brings a sense of confidence like knowing you are looking your best.

If you are interested in gaining more in-depth information and personalized training, I invite you to check out classes offered at www.finaltouchschool.com

More Than Lipstick

Moments of Meditation

What kind of first impression do you think you make? What does it say about you? Is that the message you wish to convey to others?

Do you tend to focus more on your appearance or the condition of your heart? In what areas might you be able to bring more balance to your focus?

Which of the four Style types best represents your personality?

Which Body type resembles your shape most closely?

Behavior

Civility is not a mechanical act; civility is a condition of the heart.
DEBORAH KING

*Y*our behavior encompasses everything you do. This is where etiquette and civility are demonstrated. While etiquette deals with the cultural guidelines for social interaction, civility goes to the heart of how you view and treat people.

Those who have mastered etiquette are better equipped to navigate a wider range of social and professional settings. As vital as these skills are, mastering *the rules* is not enough. We all know what it is like to be around the *etiquette police* and will do anything to avoid or limit our exposure to them. Rather than bringing a sense of harmony, a stickler to *the rules* can bring a feeling of inadequacy to those they encounter. The person who can master not only the rules of etiquette, but also the art of civility will become unstoppable.

Some may disagree, but the truth remains, your behavior at the dining table, and elsewhere, determines your level of success. Your success in business, your success in dating, and your successful job interview are largely determined by your behavior.

How would you rate your table manners, your ability to meet and greet others in a business setting, or your social skills at a formal event? One way to test your knowledge can be found on our website. We have provided a simple test which will give you a starting point to see where you may be lacking. Another suggestion I often share with my youth classes is to record or put a mirror in front of yourself while dining. This will help you see a clear picture of any behavior that may need correcting.

You can further examine your current skill level by asking yourself who taught you the manners or etiquette you currently use. Many times we do certain things without questioning why. We mirror the example of those who raised us. How many times have you done something, and when questioned you answered, "That's the way I've always done it."

Why not increase your understanding of current guidelines for social etiquette? When going into a new situation with someone from another culture, generation or gender, why not ask questions beforehand to make sure you know what is proper, or what will make the other person most comfortable?

In addition to learning solid guidelines for good etiquette, we must also strive for civility. Honestly, no one really cares what fork you use or if you can execute a perfect handshake if you are not able to cultivate healthy relationships. Consumed with daily to-do lists, we often forget to pause and really see the people with whom we are living life. Others become invisible.

Uncivil behavior is rooted in the belief that one person has greater value than another. The ability to demonstrate care for others and view each person as being made with worth and value is the heart of civility. More importantly, it is the heart of God. When we act in a manner that honors others, our actions will have a ripple effect of grace and courtesy that can make a positive impact on every person we encounter.

More Than Lipstick

Moments of Meditation

Why is it important to learn and practice good etiquette?

In what ways do you devalue others?

In what ways do you honor others?

Could practicing civility enhance your relationships?
Personally? Professionally?

Communication

Take care that you don't diminish your life to
texts, tweets, pins, and posts.
DEBORAH KING

Communication includes speech, body language, listening skills,
and the use of technology. Not only do we communicate face-to-
face, we also place phone calls, text, tweet, pin, post, and write
on each other's virtual walls. Much of our communication is done
through technology, and as wonderful as that is, it is also filled
with pitfalls. Unlike face-to-face interactions in which both people

have verbal and nonverbal cues to draw upon for understanding, technology is limited to text or images on a screen. This setting is ripe for misunderstanding and has the potential to influence far beyond the intended recipient.

Words do matter. In Proverbs it says that the tongue has the power of life and death.[2] Once an unkind comment has left my lips, it is like an arrow that pierces another's heart. Sadly, there is no delete button that can remove it. I can, and should, quickly apologize, but the wound caused by my painful remarks remains.

I find I am less likely to offend when I practice this four-step process:

1. Pause. Pausing is classy! Instead of saying the first thing that comes to my mind, I take a deep breath and wait. This is especially important when I am emotionally charged.
2. Think. How can I add value to this conversation? I carefully consider what was just said and the variety of things I could say in response.
3. Pray. I ask the Holy Spirit what He thinks about what is being said and how I should respond.
4. Speak. When my words have been filtered through this process, I am less likely to offend others and more likely to add value to the conversation.

The use of these four steps has led me to be a more effective communicator. Actively using these keys has helped me to not only hear the words which are being spoken, but *listen to the heart* for what is not being spoken. In our hurry-up world, it is common to focus more on getting our point across than listening to understand what another is saying.

When speaking with a friend or family member, how often would you be able to repeat back the words they have spoken to you? Many misunderstandings and conflicts can be avoided if we listen closely to what is being said, rather than thinking ahead to our next point in the conversation.

Not only do you want to communicate with others in a respectful and civil manner, but take time to examine how you talk to yourself. What do you say about and to yourself? Would you embrace a friend who spoke to you the way you do?

Remember to be kind to yourself. Speak to yourself the same way you would speak to your closest friends. As you do, your confidence level will increase immeasurably.

More Than Lipstick

Moments of Meditation

What is your primary method for communicating with others? Why?

Describe the benefits and drawbacks of the following: face-to-face communication; telephone conversation; email messages; text messages; social media.

How do you monitor your speech?

Do you feel you listen with your ears or with your heart most often?

Self-talk is vital to good self-esteem. Do you talk more positively or negatively to yourself? How can you improve your self-talk?

Routines

Sow a thought, and you reap an act; sow an act, and you reap a
habit; sow a habit, and you reap a character;
sow a character, and you reap a destiny.

SAMUEL SMILES

Thoughts matter. Proverbs tells us that as a woman thinks in her
heart, so is she.[3] Your thoughts reveal who you really are.

What do you think about all day? Depression, lack, fear, and
your inability? Or joy, abundance, peace, and His ability? Your
thoughts become your conversations. What are you saying? Have
you ever heard yourself say something and wondered where it came

from? The truth is; it sprang from what was in your heart. The thoughts that become part of your conversation, eventually become part of your life. That is why it is so important to continually examine your thoughts in light of God's Word.

As the prior quote by Samuel Smiles says, your thoughts become your actions, which become your routines, and in turn, those routines lead you to your destiny. At some point, you decided to do things in certain ways. Routines are those things you do day after day with little or no thought. Those daily routines become the decisions that direct your life.

I often find myself driving somewhere and realize I am headed in the wrong direction. In that moment, I recognize I am operating out of my routine or what I would call my daily *auto-pilot*. If I don't quickly adjust my course, I will end up somewhere I did not plan to go. The routines you allow will set the course for the entire day and, eventually, your life. That is why it is so important to set your *auto-pilot* for your desired destination.

Part of your daily routine includes getting dressed. Do you require five minutes, twenty minutes, one hour, or more to get ready? Do you bathe or shower? Wear make-up or prefer a bare face? Curl, straighten, or simply comb your hair? Dress formally or casually? Wear heels or flats? Whatever your preferences, your routine sets the stage for your physical appearance in the day ahead.

Just as you physically set the course for your day, what you focus your mind on will structure your thoughts for the day. You can set your thoughts on His peace and care for you, or allow your mind to wander unfocused. You can start your day filling your mind with current world events, focusing on personal conflicts and problems, or allow the Word of God to focus your thoughts on His promises. Are you spending time with God, gaining His perspective? He longs to have a conversation with you. Have you tuned your ear to hear His quiet whispers? He has much He would like to say to you.

Moments of Meditation

When you are doing your morning routine, what do you think about? What do you say to yourself; do your thoughts tend to be positive or negative?

This week, for every negative thought you catch yourself thinking, intentionally replace it with three positive thoughts. Take time to journal your observations in your *More Than Lipstick Journal.*

Body, Soul, Spirit

You are a spirit, who has a soul and lives in a body.
DEBORAH KING

God created you with a body, a soul, and a spirit. Your body is the physical house God gave you to live in here on earth. This is where your five senses—seeing, hearing, tasting, touching, and feeling—exist. Your soul is your processing center, including your mind, will, and emotions. Your spirit is the part of you that will live forever.

57

Each part of you is important and needs to be nurtured. A healthy body requires proper nutrition and exercise. A healthy soul requires education—both academic and experiential. A healthy spirit requires a personal relationship with the Lord, which includes time reading His Word and in prayer.

God has charged you with the responsibility of taking care of the body, soul and spirit He has given you. He has placed an incredibly high value on you, and He wants you to realize that value and treat yourself accordingly.

Many years ago, God gave me a wonderful, visual example of how He views our worth. I would like to share this with you, hoping it will impact you as much as it has me.

I can't resist shiny things. No matter what brings me into a shopping mall, things that glitter and shine always capture my attention and draw me to them. More often than not, it is a cluster of items displayed on a sale table or atop a glass case for shoppers to touch, fall in love with and take home. I admit, I am one of those who have to pick-up the shiny gem, try it on and admire its brilliance in a nearby mirror. After a few moments of handling it and seeing how it may look on me, I often decide to return it to the place where I found it. Why? I don't see its value.

In many stores, there are shiny baubles readily available for customers to examine. Each passing customer who picks an item up, examines and replaces it, leaves behind their fingerprints, and the item quickly loses its luster. After all, it is only an imitation. That pretty *diamond ring* is nothing more than an inexpensive cut of glass—a cubic zirconium or another man-made material—made to appear to be a diamond. While it may look pretty, it is not the real thing, and every shopper knows it.

A true diamond has a very different look and feel from an imitation. A woman often knows when she is holding the real thing, and what woman doesn't love a beautiful diamond – especially a diamond ring?

Where do you find true diamonds? True diamonds are secured behind locked cases in a jewelry store, and that shopping experience is very different. While you can peer through the glass and observe the beauty of the items inside, you are not allowed to touch the merchandise without the assistance of the jeweler.

Once you have made your selection, you point to the one you would like to try on. The jeweler takes his or her key, unlocks the case, and carefully removes the diamond ring to place on a piece of fabric for you to examine. Under the watchful gaze of the jeweler, you lift the ring, slip it onto your finger, and admire the way it looks and feels. After a moment or two, you remove the ring, place it back on the fabric and the jeweler slips it back into the case and locks the door.

Unlike the ring with a cubic zirconium, you are not allowed to touch, try on, and walk around the store alone wearing a diamond ring to see if you like it. A true diamond is only released to the person who recognizes its value and is willing to pay the price for this stunning gem.

How often have we allowed our hearts, our bodies, or our minds to be handled and damaged by those who do not embrace our true worth? How often have we allowed others to pick us up, and then quickly toss us aside? How often have we given away our beauty to one who was not willing to pay the price?

Like a flawless diamond, you have great value. You are priceless in your Father's eyes, and as you value yourself, so shall you be valued in the eyes of others. Honor your value and settle for no less than God's best. Protect your body, soul and spirit.

Moments of Meditation

What do you do to nourish your spirit? Your soul? Your body?

Do you give more attention to your body, your soul, or your spirit? In what ways can you bring balance to these areas?

How does your morning routine set the tone for the rest of the day?

Body

Imagine a world where beauty is a source
of confidence, not anxiety.
THE DOVE CAMPAIGN FOR REAL BEAUTY

Your body is a beautiful gift from God. Do you view it that way?

I think every person struggles with accepting and then embracing the body God has given him or her. I certainly have. At times, I have wished I had been given a different body, but I did not get to choose. I did not pick the shape of my nose, the size of my fingers, the shade of my skin, the length of my arms or legs, the color of my eyes, or the texture of my hair. (I did, however, select the color of my hair.)

What I do get to choose is how I will care for my body, and I don't take that responsibility lightly. Years ago I made a decision not to eat fast food or drink soda, which was not easy for me because they were regular parts of my diet. Over time I made small changes, and today I hunger for whole grains, fish, chicken, lamb, bison, fruits, nuts, vegetables, and lots of fresh water.

I never diet. The one diet I did go on in high school actually left me several pounds heavier. At that point, I decided dieting was not a good plan. How many people do you know who have gone on diets, lost the desired weight, and maintained that weight loss over a lifetime? Probably not many. More often than not, people who diet find themselves in an endless cycle of dieting, gaining weight, and dieting again. Food becomes their focus. I've found a better goal is simply to eat foods that nourish and heal my body.

Regular exercise is also a daily habit. I am not fond of working out at the gym, so I have created a workout area in my own home. Depending on my schedule for the day, I may ride my stationary bike, spend some time on the treadmill, or select one of my video workouts. While I certainly do not have an athlete's body, I do make it a priority to develop strength, flexibility, and aerobic health through my daily routine. Many factors can impact body weight, some of which are outside of a person's control. My experience is that my weight has remained stable throughout my adult life due to making healthy food choices, maintaining a daily exercise routine, and getting proper rest.

Be a good steward of the body you have been given. It is a priceless gift from God and to be treasured as you would your finest gem.

Moments of Meditation

How do you feel about the body you have?

Do you feel *comfortable in your own skin* or are there areas you are lacking confidence in? Are these areas changeable? If so, what can you do now to make your desired change?

What steps can you take to manage your health more effectively?

Soul

A noble and God-like character is not a thing of favor or chance,
but is the natural result of continued effort in right thinking, the
effect of long-cherished association with God-like thoughts.

JAMES ALLEN

Thoughts create emotions; eventually, affecting a life. This is why
I carefully guard what I see, hear, and experience each day. While
I can't control everything that happens to me in my day, there is
much I can do to maintain my mental and emotional health.

When my children were young, I enjoyed the process of
canning and freezing various foods for the winter. I remember

canning peaches for the first time. It was late August and very hot in our small two-bedroom apartment. The long hours spent peeling peaches and standing over a hot stove could have easily been exchanged for a day at the beach. I kept reminding myself that come winter, when it was cold outside and all the fresh fruit was gone, we would enjoy an abundance of yummy peaches.

Managing my thoughts is like canning peaches. I don't always feel like doing the daily work of reading the Bible, learning new skills, and managing my emotions, but it is well worth the effort when the difficult challenges of life arrive unbidden at the door of my heart. In those moments, I have the resources deep within myself to meet those challenges because I have sown them into my heart and mind.

How do you respond to challenging situations? Do you find that you repeatedly say and do things you later regret? Are your emotions overwhelming you and clouding your decisions? One definition of habit-insanity is doing the same thing over and over again, expecting different results. New results require new ways of thinking.

How do you make a real change in your life? It begins with learning a new way of thinking about a particular subject or issue. When you desire to learn a new skill, you read books, do research, or attend a structured course. Your results are based on how you think, so your source of information is vital.

More Than Lipstick

Where do you go for your information? Is it reliable? While the Internet provides instant information in the comfort of your home, is the source trustworthy? I often remind my clients that just because they found something on the Internet doesn't necessarily mean it's true!

What is your source for truth? For me, the final answer must be the Word of God found in the Bible. His Word is spirit and life.[4] When I sense my emotions overwhelming my heart and I feel my thoughts are running wild, I go to the Bible. I search for answers from His Word on whatever dilemma I am facing. His ways are perfect and will never disappoint. As I think and meditate on what He has to say about a particular issue, my mind is renewed, my thoughts begin to change, and my emotions are stilled.

Moments of Meditation

How do you respond to challenging situations?

Where do you turn first when you need an answer to a question?

Where do you turn when you feel emotionally overwhelmed?

Spirit

Real beauty creates mystery and
leaves something to be uncovered.

DEBORAH KING

*W*hile I honor and care for the body I have been given and continually challenge myself to learn new skills, my true worth is not
based on either of those things. I am created in the likeness and
image of God, and my worth is found not in my physical being,
but in my spiritual being. I am a spirit being, first and forever. My
emotions will pass, academic education is endless, and my body

will continue to fade, but my spirit will live forever. God formed me from the dust of the earth and breathed His breath into me. He gave me life. In Him I live and move and have my being![5] My life is not my own. I have been created by Him and for Him.

As I begin each day, I choose where I will place my focus. Will I place my thoughts on the temporal things which will fade away, or will I choose to place my focus on those things which are eternal? The area to which you give the most attention will be the area that flourishes. For example, if you give more focus to your soul than you do your spirit, you will find that your emotions or intellect will set the course for your day.

So often, as women, we focus much of our attention on our bodies. Younger women want to dress, talk and act older. Mature women spend millions annually on ways to appear younger. These priorities are entirely misplaced. God wants our attention focused on something much higher.

Rather than placing all your focus on how you look or how you feel, spend time feeding your spirit. Spending time reading God's Word, praying for others, reaching out with kindness and love to those in need are actions that feed your spirit.

Are you a woman who is mature in the ways of God? Then be a godly, mature woman by nurturing those who are younger. Lovingly model and embrace your current season of life by being a woman who is kind and loving; touching the hearts of those you encounter.

More Than Lipstick

Whether you are young, middle-aged or more seasoned, God has a plan for your day, your week, your month, your life. You will only truly satisfy that plan as you place the highest priority upon feeding your spirit and guarding your time with Him each day.

My daily time of preparation is a sacred time I protect. It is my time alone in prayer as I ready myself— body, soul, and spirit—for the day before me. I pray you will also draw strength from the time you set aside to spend with Him each day.

Moments of Meditation

Where do you invest the most time in preparation each day: your body, soul or spirit?

What do you do each day to feed and nurture your spirit?

Do you have a daily time of prayer? If so, describe it. If not, what can you do to begin nourishing your spirit?

Are you a woman who is mature in your relationship with God? If so, how can you influence those who are younger in the Lord?

Preparing Myself for the Day—
A Holy Preparation

The beauty of a woman is not in the clothes she wears, the figure
she carries, or the way she combs her hair.

AUDREY HEPBURN

God placed the desire for beauty in the heart of women. It was His
idea; women, the media, or our friends and families did not come up
with it. So we do not need to feel guilty for desiring to be beautiful and
to be surrounded by beautiful things. We are created for beauty.

I would like to invite you into my dressing room for a peek into
how I view this daily process, this sacred time of preparation. It is

much more than applying lipstick and mascara, styling my hair, and choosing what I will wear. These are the personal prayers that I pray each day as I take time to focus on Him and His beauty secrets.

EYES

Lord, give me eyes to see what You see, eyes that look beyond the obvious and the ability to see every person and situation as You do. May my vision be Your vision.

I fix my gaze on You.[6]

EARS

I close out all the chatter of the world and listen for Your voice. Give me ears to hear what You hear.[7] *Your words provide life and health to me.*

Your voice is the sweetest sound of all. How I long to hear You!

When You speak, I will listen. Help me to apply Your Word to every situation I will face today, because when I do, Your wisdom flows from me.

More Than Lipstick

HAIR

You keep count of every hair on my head.[8] You know when one falls out and another takes its place. There is not a detail about my life of which You are unaware.

You have crowned me with honor and given me dominion over the works of Your hands.

As freely as my hair blows in the wind, I offer myself to You, unrestrained and with overwhelming joy.

More Than Lipstick

CLOTHING

Thank You, Father, for exchanging my filthy rags for Your rich garments: the robe of righteousness and the garment of praise.[9] They are beautiful, custom-made, and priceless!

I put on Your compassion, kindness, humility, joy, gentleness, contentment, strength, and forgiveness.[10] Your love is my basic, all-purpose garment which I am never without. Your garments never go out of style and are perfect for every occasion.

LIPS

May the words of my mouth and the meditation of my heart be acceptable in Your sight, Lord.[11] I pray that the words I speak will be Your words, and every conversation I am a part of will be life-giving.

My smile is generous, full, expressive, and strong. It is a reflection of everything You have done for me.

More Than Lipstick

SHOES

The ground I walk on is holy ground, as I am continually in Your presence. I carry Your presence everywhere I go.

Direct my steps in the path You have laid out for me.[12] If I become distracted and wander off course, draw me back quickly.

Guard my steps and protect me from evil, dangerous situations. Help me to stand firm. I will not stumble, but if I do, You are there to pick me up.

Your Word lights my path and makes my way plain.[13]

FRAGRANCE

I really do like my Chanel No. 5, Lord, but I need to apply it lightly so it will not offend those around me. Some have allergies, and others simply prefer another fragrance.

But I truly love the fragrance of Your presence. It causes no allergies, and even though some think they prefer another fragrance, Yours is captivating.

As I bathe in Your presence, I soak in Your fragrance and let it permeate every part of my being.[14] It invades every situation I encounter and leaves a sweet-smelling aroma of Your love, long after I have left.

HANDS

Thank You for these hands. As individually as You have created my fingerprints, so is Your care for me. You hold me in the palm of Your hand. You caress me with Your gentle ways and lead me. Your love and care are endless.[15]

You are my defender and protect me in the face of evil.[16] *I will fear nothing. I pray that my hands deliver Your hope, help, and healing to every person I touch today.*

More Than Lipstick

POSTURE AND POISE

In You I live and move and have my being.[17] *I stand upright before You. May my posture and presence be graceful and radiate Your beauty. My movements are purposeful and sure. I am confident in Your ability to do exceedingly and abundantly more than I could ever ask or think on my own.*[18]

I walk in Your supernatural favor. Nothing can ever separate me from Your love.[19] *I am secure in You.*

MIRROR

The reflection I look for in the mirror is not of my physical body and all the things I dislike; I look to see Your image.

I am Your daughter, created in Your image.[20] *Before the foundation of the world, You made me with a plan and a purpose.*[21] *You love me. I am Your delight. I am a reflection of You.*

DAILY SCHEDULE

The appointments of my day are not random appointments to fill my calendar or consume my moments. They are set in place by You, Lord.

Your plans are what I desire because they will never disappoint. You have ordered my steps. Every encounter I have today has divine purpose. Woven into each moment is a message, a lesson, an opportunity. Help me to make the most of every opportunity You bring my way. Remind me that the people and situations that appear to be distractions are actually a part of Your purpose. You are working all things for my good.[22]

When I prepare myself for the day in this manner, it is a holy preparation—a time of worship—not of myself, but of the King.

More Than Lipstick

Moments of Meditation

What can you do to improve your daily morning routine?

How does your morning routine prepare your body, soul, and spirit for the day ahead?

You may want to use your *More Than Lipstick Journal* to write your own prayers in your own words. Use these prayers each morning over a period of time to see what difference this makes in your life.

Popularity

Invest in character development
rather than reputation protection.
DEBORAH KING

$\mathcal{M}$any use appearance as a way to gain popularity. But, is popularity the goal? What are you seeking? Are you seeking popularity with a particular group, or are you seeking His purpose for your life?

While we all desire to be liked and included in a group, when we strive for popularity, we usually find it is always just beyond our grasp. The continual chasing, people-pleasing behavior and struggling to measure up always leave us feeling empty.

Years ago a friend asked me if I would like to see her pet raccoon. Until that day, I did not know people had pet raccoons, so I was curious to see this unusual house pet. The inquisitive critter was quite entertaining and fun to watch.

"Would you like to see him eat cotton candy?" she asked.

"Of course," I replied. How could I pass up such an opportunity?

She pulled a large chunk of bright blue cotton candy from a plastic bag and handed it to the raccoon. He eagerly put out both paws and grasped his tasty treat.

I quickly learned that raccoons wash their food before they eat it, which is not a bad policy. But, as the raccoon carefully washed the cotton candy, it slowly disappeared. Frantically, the raccoon searched for his sugary treat.

Like the raccoon and his cotton candy, popularity with people is an illusion that vanishes before your eyes and leaves you empty and alone. One moment you think you hold it; the next, it is gone.

When you hunger and seek after the presence of God, you will never be disappointed. He will always be there, and He will always satisfy your hunger for love and acceptance.

More Than Lipstick

Moments of Meditation

In what ways do you seek approval from others?

How do you handle being excluded from a group?

Take a moment and allow God to include you, to tell you how He feels about you. Let Him satisfy your hunger for love and acceptance with His presence.

$\mathcal{P}urpose$

I believe I am here for a reason, and
my purpose is greater than the challenges I face.
DEBORAH KING

$\mathcal{I}$ spend a great deal of time driving in unfamiliar places, and I do everything I possibly can to avoid arriving at my destinations late. Due to necessity, I have become very good at reading maps for navigation.

When GPS technology came on the scene, I thought it would be the greatest tool ever, and most of the time it is. However, there are two issues with GPS I find frustrating.

First, I can only see the next turn on the map and am unable to see the big picture.

Second, and even more frustrating, my GPS has taken me on routes that were not the most efficient and, at times, to places I never intended to go.

I like to see the big picture when I travel because it enables me to identify my current position, see my destination, and choose the best travel route.

I am the same way in life. I have an enormous need to see the big picture. It helps me to put everything into perspective and make sense out of my journey. Self-inflicted detours and break-downs frustrate me.

God's Word is my road map for life. It provides me with the big picture and puts my life into perspective. When I spend too much time focused on a particular moment in my journey, I am either elated with joy for my current delightful place or depressed by the difficult challenges I face.

Purpose provides the big picture for life. When you understand your purpose, your life has direction, meaning, and fullness; you find true significance.

The ultimate purpose is to know who you are and Whose you are! You are His precious daughter. He adores you. He delights in you—just as you are. He gave His all for you.

More Than Lipstick

Moments of Meditation

Describe your purpose in life.

Do you have a clear view of the big picture for your life? How would you describe your journey toward your purpose?

How does seeing or not seeing the big picture affect your daily life?

What moments have gotten you off track? What moments have served to spur you on?

Designer Original

Why be a cheap imitation of someone else
when you are a designer original?
DEBORAH KING

*H*andbags come in all sizes, shapes, colors, and materials. There
are handbags for everyday purposes, and some that are reserved for
special occasions. Some handbags are designer originals, but most
are cheap imitations. While an imitation may look like the real deal
from a distance, a trained eye can easily identify an original. Why
would someone purchase an imitation instead of an original? That

is easy—designer bags cost much more than imitations because they are investments!

You are a designer original! There never has been—nor will there ever be—another person just like you. Sadly, many people choose to be cheap imitations of others, hiding the beauty of who they truly are.

Before the foundation of the world God knew you and made you with a plan and purpose. You are a designer original, and He made the ultimate investment to purchase you: He gave His only Son for you.[23] You are His priceless treasure. You are irreplaceable. Why then do you spend so much time trying to imitate others, when you are a one-of-a-kind designer original?

We all long to feel special. We long for peace, love, contentment, significance and joy. We long to feel beautiful and unique. We will not find what we are looking for at the mall on a sale rack or a designer rack. We will not find it in the latest jar of miracle face cream or the latest cosmetic procedure. We will not find it in more jewelry, a new car, home or exotic vacation. We will not find it in a man, a best friend, or our children. Yet, we still try to find what we need outside of ourselves...and outside of Him.

You will only find your purpose and destiny in Him. He is the lover of your soul. He is your best friend; He is beauty. He is all you need to be fulfilled. In the moments you fully walk in this truth, you are whole and truly beautiful.

More Than Lipstick

God does not call you to perfection, but He does call you to His purpose. It takes strength and courage to pursue Him and do what He has placed in your heart to do. You must first know who He is, and who you are in Him. You are a mighty woman of God! You are His beloved daughter.

Esther privately and patiently prepared, and when her time came, she was ready. She understood that her true beauty was much more than applied lipstick. On the day she was summoned to go before the king, she entered as an ordinary girl and left as a queen. As queen, she was positioned for God to use her to save the Jewish people.

If the King lives within you, every day is a day of sacred preparation, not for your glory, but to take the King of kings to the world.

Moments of Meditation

In what ways have you attempted to imitate others? What effect has that had on you? Has it been positive or negative? Why?

How might seeing yourself as a "designer original" change the way you live?

Have your preparations for your calling and purpose included learning not just how to do something, but learning who you are? If not, how can you begin to pursue learning who you really are?

Does the King live within you? If not, would you like Him to? Jesus is standing at the door of your heart and longs for a personal relationship with you. Simply open your heart and invite Him to come in.[24]

Final Thoughts

As women, we fill many roles throughout the changing seasons of our lives. We are daughters, sisters, friends, wives, mothers, grandmothers, employees, employers, entrepreneurs, and volunteers, but one role that is ever constant is our position as daughter of the King. Too often, we let the pressures of our relationships and the cares of life distract us from the only One who is able to meet our every need.

I am so thankful that God's love does not depend upon how hard I work or on my being perfect. He always has and always will adore me, just as He does you. He longs for an intimate love relationship with each one of us.

More Than Lipstick

It is my prayer that every moment of your day, you will embrace Him and allow Him to be the Lover of your soul. As you do, you will experience beauty that never fades and the greatest love story ever imagined!

You shall also be so beautiful and prosperous, as to be thought of as a crown of glory and honor in the hand of the Lord, and a royal diadem—exceedingly beautiful—in the hand of your God. Isaiah 62:3 (Amp)

Moments of Meditation

What roles do you currently fill? How do you view these roles?

In what ways do you strive to be perfect?

How do you reflect His beauty every day?

What is the next step in preparation for your true calling? It might be that you need to pursue freedom from past labels, wounds, or thoughts. It might be that you need to pursue a relationship with the King who has designed you as a unique original, and truly has your best in mind. Take some time to pursue His thoughts and opinions about you. He is always good! Be sure to journal the thoughts and feelings you encounter as you pursue His presence.

Scripture References

Unless otherwise noted, all scriptures are from the Holy Bible: New International Version. For the complete story of Esther, see the book of Esther in the Bible.

---

1. Esther 1:2–12
2. Proverbs 18:21
3. Proverbs 27:19; 23:7 (NKJV)
4. John 6:63
5. Acts 17:28
6. Psalms 119:15 (ESV)
7. Proverbs 20:12
8. Matthew 10:30
9. Isaiah 61:3–10
10. Colossians 3:12
11. Psalms 19:14
12. Proverbs 3:6; Psalms 119:133; Proverbs 16:9
13. Psalms 119:105
14. Acts 2:28
15. Jeremiah 31:3
16. Psalms 62:2 (NET)
17. Acts 17:28
18. Ephesians 3:20
19. Romans 8:39
20. Genesis 1:26
21. Jeremiah 29:11
22. Romans 8:28
23. John 3:16
24. Revelation 3:20

Deborah King Live

Would you like to learn from Deborah King in person? Are you interested in learning more about how you can enhance your personal style, behavior, dining and conversational skills? You can! Deborah leads a variety of programs on image, civility and etiquette for youth and adults which are open to the general public. Deborah is also available for personal coaching and corporate training. You can view the current class descriptions and scheduling on her website.

If you would like to arrange a private program for your group or have Deborah speak at your next event, you can email her at Deborah@ finaltouchschool.com.

Additional Educational Resources from Deborah King
More Than Lipstick Journal
More Than Lipstick Note Cards
More Than Lipstick Bookmark
More Than Lipstick Bible Study Guide
More Than Lipstick Book, Spanish version
Young Ladies and Gentlemen Web-based Training for Children
Caught in the Act Civility Cards
Etiquette Flash Cards

For More Information Contact:
Deborah King, AICI CIP, CPC, CPECP
Final Touch Finishing School, Inc.
www.finaltouchschool.com
Deborah@finaltouchschool.com
(206) 510-5357

For more tips, thoughts and inspiration,
you will enjoy Deborah's blog,
What Would Mrs. King Do? – www.whatwouldmrskingdo.com

About the Author

Deborah King is a wife, mother, and president of Final Touch Finishing School, Inc.—the premier finishing school in the United States. Final Touch Finishing School was founded by Deborah in Seattle, Washington, in 1989. Her passion is to equip people from all walks of life with the necessary skills to move confidently from the informal to the formal with ease and grace. She teaches how to evaluate each social and business circumstance, as well as how to respond with appropriate poise and manners based on a variety of cultural considerations.

Deborah's influence and experience in the civility, etiquette, and image industry has spanned decades, and she serves as a reliable resource to the media. Deborah travels extensively, both domestically and internationally, teaching principles of etiquette and poise to individuals aged five to seventy-five. Hailed as the *Queen of Etiquette & Civility*, Deborah's warm teaching style is based on the simplicity of kindness and respect for self, others, and property. Her programs instill a greater sense of potential and increased confidence for all who attend. A native of Seattle, Washington, she currently resides near Dallas, Texas.

FINAL TOUCH FINISHING SCHOOL

Developing the skills for life since 1989.

Final Touch Finishing School, Inc., is the premier finishing school in the United States. For over 25 years, Final Touch has led the way in teaching women and men, girls and boys, how to move from informal to formal situations with ease and grace.

FINAL TOUCH
FINISHING SCHOOL, INC.

DEBORAH KING

(206) 510-5357
www.finaltouchschool.com
PO Box 142 · Decatur, TX 76234

Made in the USA
Charleston, SC
16 April 2015